AF393026

This book
belongs to:

____

____

____

____

First published 2023 with an exclusive licence from the author to CHEETAH® Purrrrrrr Publishing, an imprint of CHEETAH® Toys & More, LLC (CHEETAH®).

Contact us: 1-860-781-1276, 1-876-909-6311 (WhatsApp),
info@mycheetahacademy.com; paulettetrowers@yahoo.com

ISBN-13: 979-8-3303-5020-9
ISBN-10: 8-3303-5020-9

Dear CHEETAH® family:

Our little books were specially created to help our early readers master their decoding skills and build reading fluency. The repetitive use of high-frequency words, word families, decodable words, rhymes, and vivid illustrations facilitates this process. Our stories complement the objectives and content highlighted in the Jamaica Early Childhood Curriculum Guide and the Ministry of Education and Youth Grade 1 National Standards Curriculum.

In journeying through our series, our little ones will develop a deeper awareness of, and appreciation for, our Jamaican culture. Our books also have universal appeal, as any early reader can identify with the characters, events and subjects in our texts. Readers will get to enjoy the stories, build vocabulary, and exercise critical thinking by engaging in the activities at the end of each story.

Additionally, as a precursor to our series, or as a support to it, we've created a decodable 'sentence strip' book for the very young readers and those who require more scaffolding.

Happy reading!

CHEETAH®

Chasing and capturing your dreams with you.

Learning the alphabet is like unlocking the secrets of a magical book filled with surprises. Let's go! Let's unlock the secrets of the magical book!

My decodable words:

can, van, flat, mat, that, Ben,
get, set, big, jig, pig, wig,
fin, win, bit, sit, fun, run

Letter sounds:

- Consonant digraph sound /w/ in the initial and final positions in words.

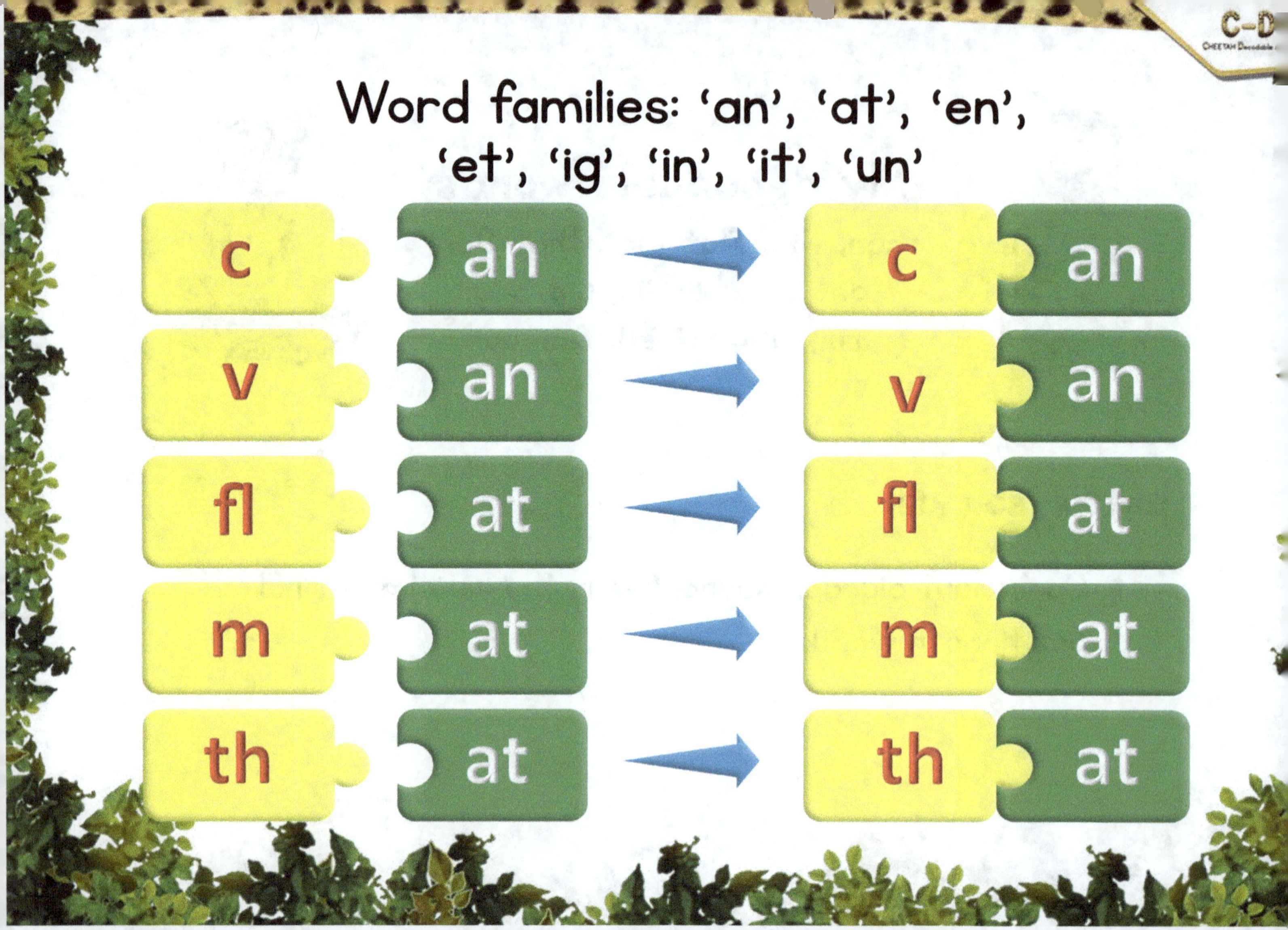

Word families: 'an', 'at', 'en', 'et', 'ig', 'in', 'it', 'un'
c an → c an
v an → v an
fl at → fl at
m at → m at
th at → th at

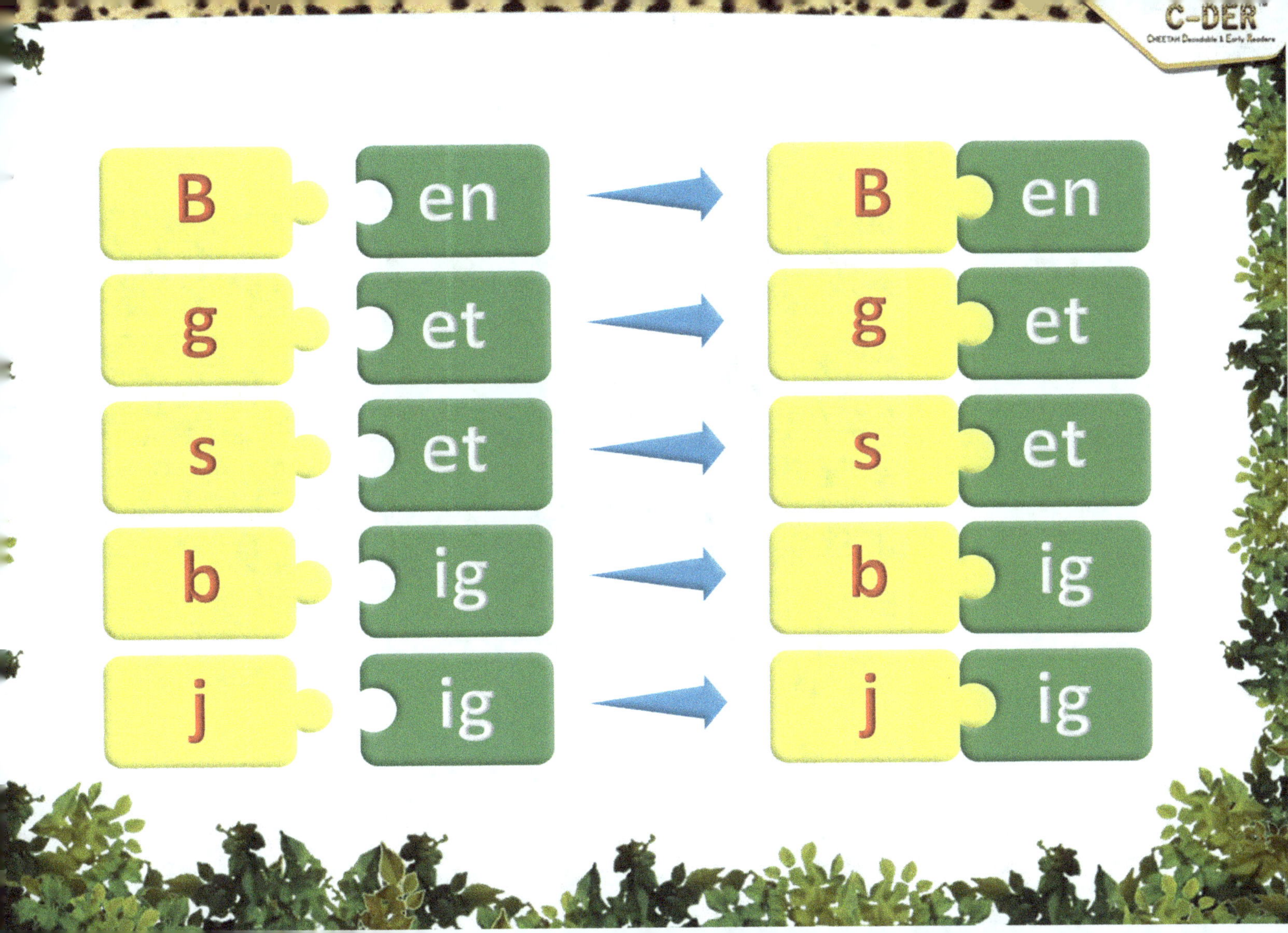
C-DER
B en
g et
s et
b ig
j ig
B en
g et
s et
b ig
j ig

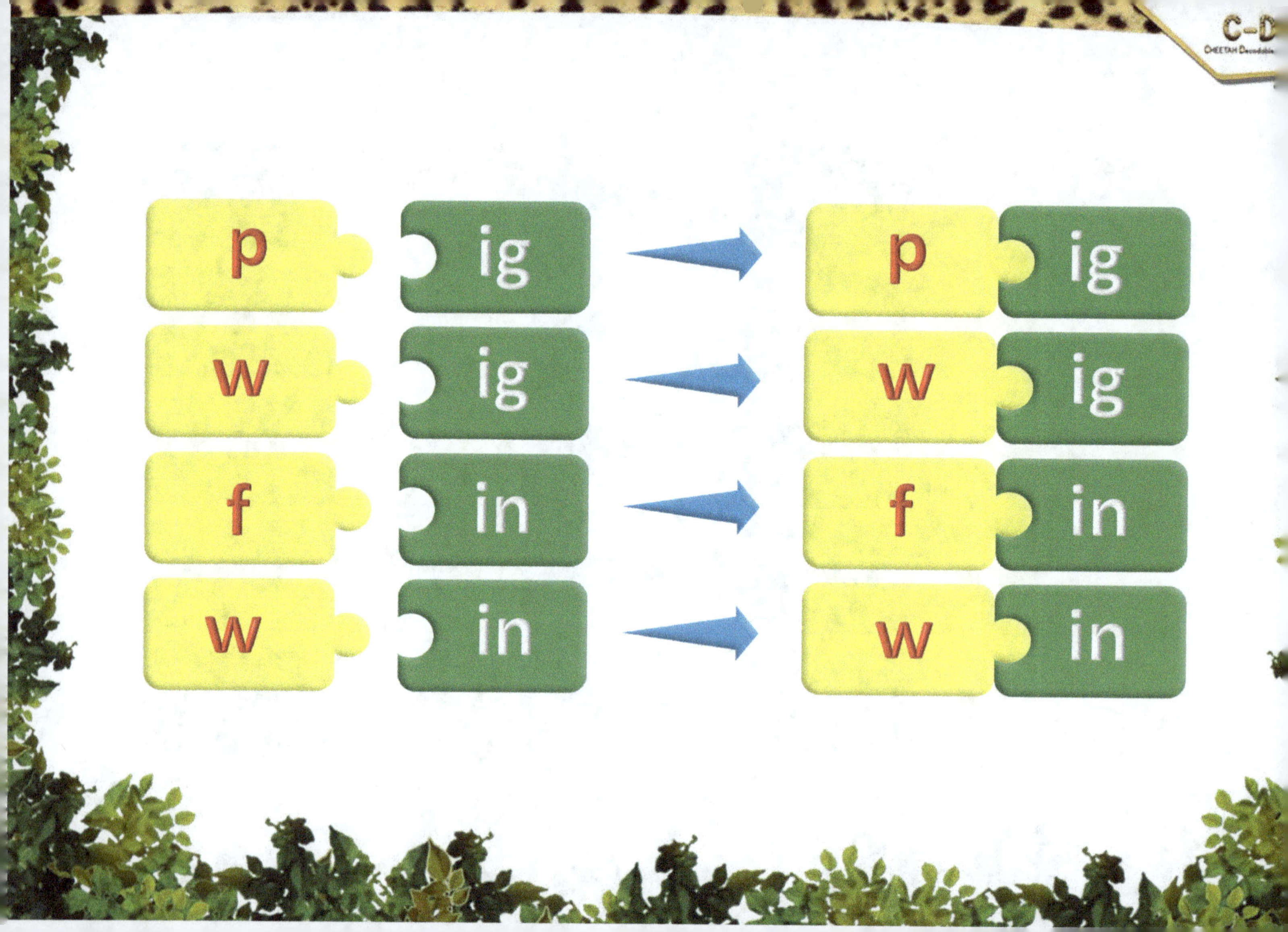
p
ig
p ig
w
ig
w ig
f
in
f in
w
in
w in

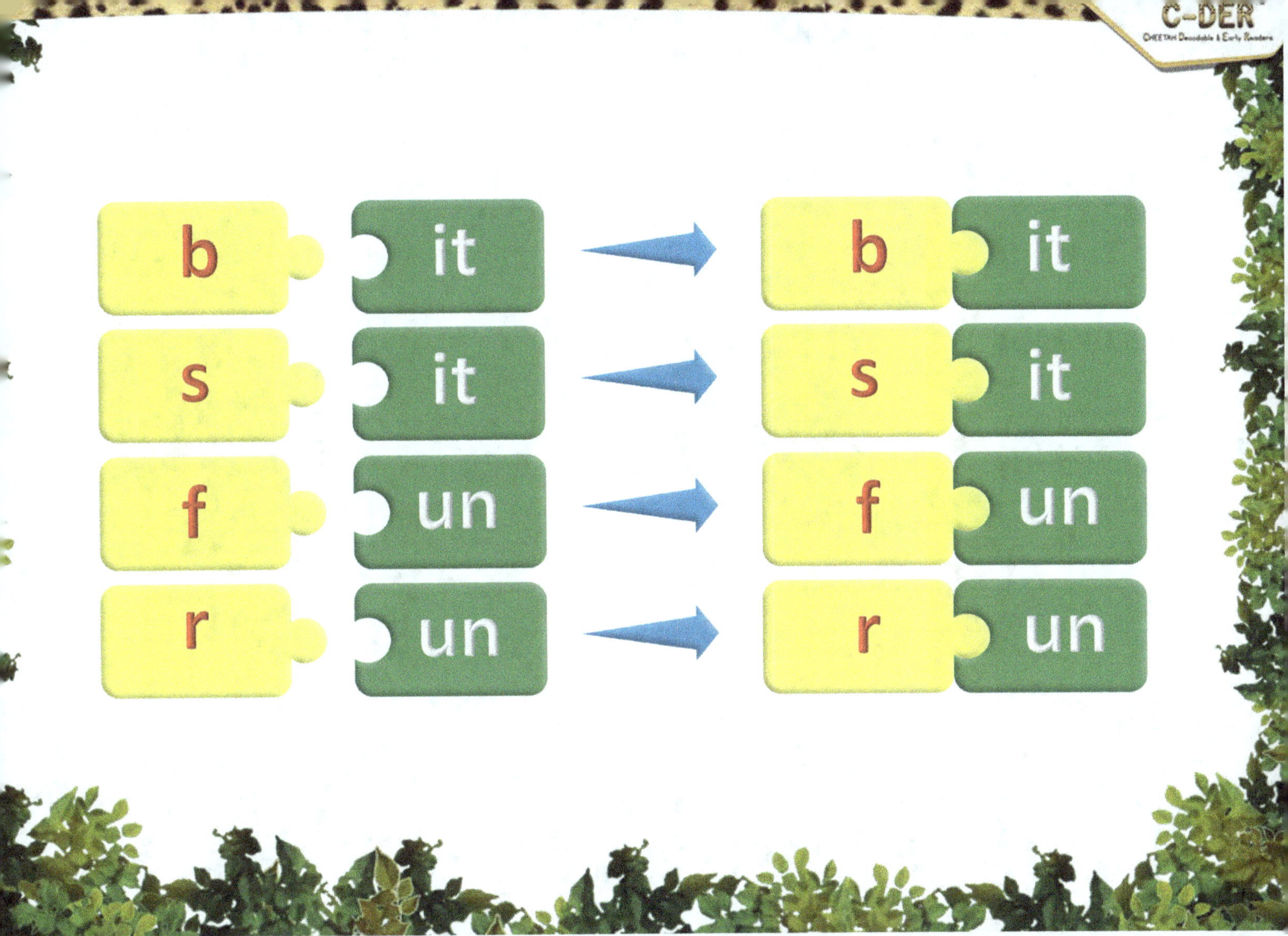

b
it
b it

s
it
s it

f
un
f un

r
un
r un

'Mom, what can I wear? It is "dress-up" day.

If I wear this wig, what will my friends say?

What do you think? Do you think I will win?

Or...

Should I dress like a fish and wear a fin?'

'I think you will look nice in the wig,
but it is a little bit big.
And...
a fin will look good on you.
I think you will be a good fish too!'

4

'hmmmm...I think I will dress up as a
pig,
and to be funny, I will wear a wig.
I can do a little jig.
Yes, I think I will dress up as a pig.'

7

'Well,' says Mom, 'Get set. We are late.

Daddy is waiting in the van by the gate.'

Wendy wears an all-pink suit.

She wears pink boots that are very cute.

Wendy wears the big yellow wig.

She does not mind that it is big.

Dad takes her to school. She walks past the gate.

Wendy runs to class. She is very late.

11

'Hello Wendy,' says Miss Brown.

Miss Brown is dressed up as a clown.

Miss Brown says to Wendy, 'Please sit.

It will be your turn in a little bit.'

Dress up day

They all look at Ben who is on the mat.

Ben is on his tummy. He lies flat.

Ben is dressed up as a white whale.

He looks good with his big white tail.

Dress up day
15

Wendy walks up next. She does a jig.

She looks very funny in her yellow wig.

The children laugh, and so does the clown.

Wouldn't you love a teacher as fun as Ms. Brown?

Discussion and activities:

1. Have the children share their experiences of a time that they had to 'dress-up' for school in a costume or some special outfit other than their uniform.

2. Have the children identify the words with the target letter and sound.

3. Have the children make the sound of the target letter and identify rhyming words in the text.

Discussion and activities:

4. Discuss the words: cute and jig as used in the context of the story.

5. Have the children read the text aloud.

Questions:

1. What special day or celebration do you think the children are 'dressing-up' for in the story?

2. Do you think that the children in the story like dress-up day? What makes you think so?